The Mosaic of My Journey

Ravee S Aahluwalia

Qurate
qauratebooks.com

The Mosaic of My Journey
Ravee S Aahluwalia

Published in 2024

© Published by

Qurate Books Pvt. Ltd.
Goa 403523, India
www.quratebooks.com
Tel: 1800-210-6527, Email: info@quratebooks.com

ISBN: 978-93-58981-27-8

Preface

Life is an extraordinary journey, a beautiful mosaic of moments, relationships, and experiences that shape who we are and who we are destined to become. As I pen these pages, I am overwhelmed with gratitude for the people who have been integral to my journey. This book is not just a recounting of my story—it is a reflection of the countless lessons, relationships, and insights that have guided me, shaped me, and helped me grow.

First and foremost, I dedicate this work to my wife, Nidhi, whose unwavering love and support have been the bedrock of my life. To my lovely children, Aadishwar and Eekisha, you are the purest embodiment of joy and hope, inspiring me every single day to strive for better. Your laughter, love, and light fill my heart in ways words cannot describe.

I extend my heartfelt gratitude to my father and mother, whose sacrifices and values laid the foundation of my life. To my in-laws, who welcomed me with open arms and supported me unconditionally, thank you for being part of my story.

To my family and friends, I owe a deep debt of gratitude for standing by me through the highs and lows, for believing in my dreams when they seemed far-fetched, and for being my cheerleaders in moments of doubt.

A special mention goes to my life friend over the ages, Roopa, whose wisdom, guidance, and unwavering belief in me have been nothing short of divine. She has been my chariot, my anchor, and the light that has dispelled darkness during some of my most challenging times. Her ability to restore my self-worth and inspire me to embrace my purpose has been one of the greatest blessings of my life.

I cannot forget Wavell, my birthday twin and confidant, whose loyalty, courage, and unwavering support have been a lifeline. He has stood by me without hesitation, offering strength and conviction when I needed it most. Wavell is the kind of person who embodies unconditional friendship and trust—a bond that goes beyond words.

To Aman, Tony, Puneet, Karan, Sonu, Anmol, Harpreet, Sachin, Vikas, Vishav, Ginni, Shenti, Sonia Didi, Abhinandan, Amit, Atul, Vibhoo, Rahul, Sukhi, Rohit, Tariq, Gogi, Anwar, Vijay Sai, JP Singh, and Jagatjit Singh, your unwavering camaraderie and presence in my life have added countless shades of joy and resilience to my journey. Each of you has contributed to shaping the person I am today, and for that, I am eternally grateful.

To the countless people I have interacted with over the years—teachers, mentors, colleagues, friends, and even strangers—you have all been my guides. Every conversation, every experience, every challenge has been a lesson, and this book is a testament to the profound impact you have had on my journey.

As I recount the stories and milestones that define my life, my hope is that this book resonates with you. I hope it inspires you to embrace your own journey with love, courage, and gratitude. Life, after all, is lived in the present moment—the only reality we truly have. Let us honor it, celebrate it, and live it to its fullest potential.

With love and gratitude,
Ravee S Aahluwalia

Introduction

Freedom. It's a word that stirs something deep within us—a yearning, a desire, a call to live on our own terms. But what does it truly mean to be free? As a young boy stepping out of the structured confines of school, I believed freedom meant escaping routine and responsibility. To me, it was about spreading my wings, embracing life without boundaries, and chasing the thrill of the moment.

As life unfolded, however, I discovered a truth that reshaped my understanding of freedom. It's not about running away from responsibility or chasing fleeting pleasures. True freedom lies in the ability to align your actions with your aspirations, to live a life that resonates with your values and dreams.

This book is a journey through those lessons. It is a chronicle of the struggles, failures, realizations, and transformations that have shaped the person I am today. It's about the people who entered my life as guides, the challenges that became opportunities, and the moments of clarity that emerged when I learned to live fully in the present.

Through these pages, I hope to share the essence of what I've learned—that life's most profound gifts often come wrapped in adversity, and the key to embracing them lies in trusting the journey. Above all, this book emphasizes the transformative power of the present moment. It is in the "NOW" that life's lessons unfold, where true freedom resides, and where clarity, joy, and purpose are found.

This is not just my story; it's an invitation for you to reflect on your own path, embrace the present, and rediscover the freedom that comes from living authentically and courageously.

Contents

Chapter 1

Out of the Cage

I was just out of school, finally free from the maddening race to be first in class and the relentless grind of board exams. College brought with it an intoxicating sense of freedom—a break from the monotonous routine of endless studying and little else. For the first time, I felt I could breathe, explore, and live without the looming shadow of expectations.

But in my eagerness to embrace this newfound freedom, I drifted far from the realities of life and the practicalities everyone expected of me. My family, my teachers, and even my peers all seemed to echo the same refrain: "Focus on your career." Yet, I was consumed by something entirely different—a curiosity about myself and the world around me.

During this time, I developed a fascination for someone who had been my junior in school. She became the focal point of my days. I found excuses to stroll through her street, made friends with people in her neighborhood, and sought fleeting moments where I could simply see her or be near her. In those moments, I wasn't thinking about the future or the expectations weighing on me. I was completely, unabashedly present—immersed in a world of raw emotions and fleeting glances, where nothing else seemed to matter.

Chapter 2

Narrowing the Vision

Life seemed perfect, or so I convinced myself. I had settled into a routine that revolved around her, and for a while, that was enough. It didn't matter that my world had shrunk or that my goals had taken a backseat. I was happy, or so I thought.

But life has a way of shaking you awake when you least expect it. The shock came one afternoon when she told me she was leaving. Her family had decided she would move to her grandparents' house, 150 kilometers away, to focus on her medical entrance exams. She had already enrolled in tutorial classes there, and her plans were set.

Her words hit me like a blow. I felt the ground shift beneath me, and suddenly, the world I had so carefully constructed began to crumble. My mind raced. How would I manage without seeing her every day? How would I cope with the distance? I wasn't just losing her physical presence—I was losing the fragile sense of purpose I had tied so tightly to her.

Driven by these feelings, I made a decision that felt right in the moment but would later haunt me. I chose to enroll in a B.Sc. Non-Medical program at the local college, not because it aligned with my aspirations, but because it allowed me to stay close to her. I convinced myself it was the right choice, that being near her was reason enough.

For a while, it felt fulfilling. I saw her almost every day. I found excuses to linger in her presence, even if it was just a passing glance or a brief exchange of words. It gave me a sense of purpose, though it was a fleeting and hollow one. I mistook proximity for progress, affection for accomplishment. Looking back, I see now how much I had confined myself to a narrow vision, losing sight of my own potential.

Chapter 3

Clinging to the Illusion

Despite the growing weight of reality pressing at the edges of my consciousness, I continued my daily routine of visiting her. Each morning, I would set out, traveling the 150 kilometers to her new town. I would wait outside her tutorial classes, eager for the fleeting moments we could share when she stepped out. Those brief interactions, those stolen minutes, felt like my lifeline. They were enough to keep me going—or so I thought.

I told myself that this was love, that my unwavering presence was an act of devotion. It felt fulfilling in its own way. But deep down, I knew something was amiss. My insecurities whispered fears I couldn't ignore. What if she grew distant? What if this new environment and these new friendships pulled her further away from me? These thoughts gnawed at the edges of my mind, but I dismissed them, clinging to the illusion that proximity would solve everything.

My entire world revolved around her. I had no clear path, no ambitions outside of being near her. But as time passed, cracks began to form in the foundation of this fragile reality. Those cracks widened the day she confronted me with a question I wasn't prepared to answer.

Chapter 4

The Awakening

It was an ordinary day, or so I thought. We were talking as usual when she looked at me, her gaze steady and serious, and asked, "Why aren't you serious about your life? About your career? What's your plan after completing your B.Sc.? What have you thought about for your future?"

Her words felt like a slap. I stumbled for a response, but none came. I had no plan, no ambition beyond her. My life had become a blank canvas, with every brushstroke dictated by her presence. She saw through it all, and what she said next would change everything.

"I need to make this clear to you," she said firmly. "I'm preparing for my medical entrance exams, and if I clear them and have the chance to study in Pune or down south, I won't think twice about leaving. My career is my priority, not you. All my energy is focused on this goal."

Her words hit me like a hammer. For so long, I had poured every ounce of my energy, time, and love into this one-sided relationship. I thought my devotion would be enough, that it would anchor her to me. But in that moment, I realized the truth: I was not her priority. I never had been.

Chapter 5

The Eye-Opener

The drive back home that evening was a blur. Her words played on a loop in my mind, each repetition cutting deeper than the last. It felt like the end of the road—not just with her, but with the life I had built around her. I had sacrificed opportunities, turned down my father's offer to fund my engineering education, all because I couldn't bear to leave Patiala and her. And now, I was left with nothing.

The pain of disappointment was unbearable. It felt as though everything I had invested—my time, my effort, my emotions—had been wasted. But somewhere in the depths of that despair, a small voice emerged. It whispered words of acceptance, urging me to forgive myself for the choices I had made.

That night, as I lay in bed, I confronted my reality. For the first time, I saw the problem clearly: it wasn't her honesty or even her priorities. It was my lack of clarity, my unwillingness to take control of my own life. I had allowed my feelings to dictate my actions, ignoring the need for personal growth and ambition.

Chapter 6

A Conscious Decision

As the darkness of the night gave way to the first light of morning, a sense of calm settled over me. I told myself that I couldn't change the past, but I could change how I moved forward. Her words, though painful, had opened my eyes to the imbalance in my life. I realized that the love and energy I had given to her needed to be redirected—first and foremost, to myself.

That night marked a turning point. It wasn't just the end of a relationship; it was the beginning of a new journey. One where I would prioritize my own growth, my own ambitions. For the first time, I felt conscious—spiritually and emotionally—of the path I needed to take. I didn't have all the answers yet, but I knew one thing: the life I had been living was over. A new chapter awaited, one where I would finally take charge of my destiny.

Chapter 7

Reflection

Sometimes, the most painful moments are the ones that wake us up. Her honesty shattered my illusions, but it also freed me from them. For the first time, I understood that love cannot be forced, and closeness does not guarantee connection. True love—whether for another person or yourself—is built on mutual respect, understanding, and growth.

That night, I forgave myself for my mistakes and resolved to move forward with clarity and purpose. It was the beginning of a transformation, one that would shape the person I was destined to become.

Looking back, I can now see how that moment was a catalyst for the personal growth and resilience that would define my life. It taught me the importance of self-awareness and the strength that lies in embracing hard truths. It was not just an end, but the beginning of a journey toward becoming the person I was meant to be.

Chapter 8

A New Beginning

The next morning, I woke up with a glimmer of hope. As I sipped my morning tea and scanned the newspaper, my eyes fell on a notice from the Private Engineering College Associations. The advertisement stated that due to certain legal issues, they would be conducting an all-India entrance exam to fill 50 percent of their seats on merit, while the remaining 50 percent would be allocated through capitation fees. It was already the end of the first semester, and such an opportunity was rare.

For reasons I could not fully explain, it felt as though the universe had once again opened a door for me. This was my chance to change my path and take a step toward reclaiming my future.

I grabbed this chance with both hands. Without wasting any time, I took admission and resolved to give my absolute best from that moment onward. This marked the start of a new chapter in my life—one where I decided to move forward with clarity, purpose, and unwavering determination to make the most of what had been offered to me.

Chapter 9

The Turning Point

Looking back now, that morning was the start of a new, conscious journey. It was a moment that marked a shift in my mindset and my approach to life. I began to live each moment with intention, valuing the opportunities that came my way and understanding the importance of aligning my actions with my goals.

That decision to take control of my destiny was a turning point. It taught me the power of resilience, of believing in second chances, and of trusting that the universe has a way of guiding us—if only we are willing to listen and act. This journey was no longer about anyone else; it was about me finding my path and reclaiming my life.

Chapter 10

Parallel Paths

I wanted to give my 100 percent to the most precious gift the universe had given me: my self-respect. With that thought driving me, I threw myself wholeheartedly into my studies and college life. But as I worked to reclaim my own path, news from back home shook me once again.

The girl for whom I had almost given up everything had also cleared her entrance exams and had secured admission into one of the state's most prestigious government medical colleges. It wasn't in our hometown; she would be staying in a hostel there. Part of me was genuinely happy for her. This was her dream, and she had worked hard to achieve it. But another part of me—the insecure, fearful part—was triggered again. The thought of her moving further away, meeting new people, and building a new life without me left me anxious and panicked.

I reached out to her, trying to maintain a connection despite the growing distance. This marked the beginning of a long-distance relationship. Mobile phones weren't yet common, so we relied on daily 10-minute calls through STD PCO booths. I carved out those minutes religiously, never missing a call, no matter the cost.

Managing this long-distance relationship brought new challenges. My monthly allowance from home was Rs. 2000, which barely covered my lodging, food, and college expenses. Adding the cost of daily calls meant I needed to find ways to stretch every rupee. I started taking up small projects—a total of 18 over time—to supplement my income. These weren't always concrete or reliable, but they were necessary to make ends meet.

Despite these challenges, I lived life king-size. It's only now, in hindsight, that I realize how much the universe provided for me. Resources seemed to appear just when I needed them, as if by magic. For this, I am ever grateful.

Chapter 11

Contrasting Worlds

While I was consumed by my efforts to keep the relationship alive, she seemed completely at peace. She was committed to her studies, focused, and self-assured. She had given me complete freedom and space—a stark contrast to my constant need for reassurance. Her attitude baffled me. I couldn't understand why she wasn't as anxious as I was, why she didn't seem to fear losing me.

Her calmness was unsettling. It made me question the foundation of our relationship and, more importantly, my own insecurities. I couldn't see it then, but her self-completeness was a strength I needed to learn from. She wasn't aloof; she was grounded in herself in a way that I wasn't.

Chapter 12

Lessons in Gratitude

Through all the struggles of balancing college, managing expenses, and navigating my emotions, one thing remained constant: the universe's unwavering support. Whether it was finding extra money for a call or completing a project on time, everything seemed to fall into place. Looking back, I see those moments as lessons in gratitude, reminders that even in the chaos, I was never truly alone.

A pivotal figure during this time was Kantesh, the person who ran the PCO from where I made those daily calls. Over time, he became a friend, sensing my financial situation and quietly offering me credit for months. Despite enduring his father's disapproval and frequent scolding for extending emotional leeway to clients, Kantesh continued to help without hesitation. His generosity, despite his own limited resources, was a lifeline I didn't fully appreciate at the time. I took his help for granted and never thanked him while I had the chance.

Years later, when I tried to find him to express my gratitude, I learned that his journey in this life had ended. It was a heart-wrenching realization but also a profound lesson. Kantesh exemplified how to live a life of magnanimity and service, even when resources are scarce. His story inspired me deeply, and the ethos of selfless service he embodied became the foundation of my social organization. His life taught me the value of giving without expecting anything in return—a principle I strive to uphold in every initiative I undertake.

This phase of my life taught me resilience, resourcefulness, and the value of self-reliance. It was a period of growth, not just academically but emotionally and spiritually. I began to see life not as something that happened to me but as something I had the power to shape—one decision, one action at a time.

Chapter 13

Breaking the Cycle

Life at college had become a delicate balancing act. On one hand, I was navigating the academic pressures and financial constraints of engineering life. On the other, I was wrestling with the emotional weight of maintaining a long-distance relationship. Each day felt like a new challenge, and though I kept moving forward, I often wondered how long I could sustain the pace.

The calls with her continued every evening, like clockwork. They became my anchor in the whirlwind of responsibilities and uncertainty. But they were also a mirror, reflecting back my growing insecurities. I started to realize that despite my efforts, I was caught in a cycle—constantly looking outward for validation and reassurance, yet never feeling truly secure or complete within myself.

Chapter 14

A Moment of Clarity

The moment of clarity came unexpectedly during a casual conversation with a classmate. We were discussing future goals and ambitions, and he said something that struck me deeply: "You can't pour from an empty cup. If you're not full, how will you ever give to anyone else?"

His words lingered in my mind long after the conversation ended. They forced me to confront a hard truth: I was trying to build a life around someone else without first building a solid foundation for myself. I had spent so much time chasing love and security that I had neglected the most important relationship of all—the one with myself.

Chapter 15

Turning Inward

For the first time, I began to turn inward. I started small, carving out time each day to reflect and reconnect with myself. I explored activities that brought me joy and fulfillment beyond academics and relationships. I discovered the meditative power of storytelling, weaving my thoughts into stories as a way to process my emotions. I found solace in long walks around the campus, where I could clear my mind and simply be.

These small practices became my lifeline. Slowly, they helped me shift my focus from what I lacked to what I had, from what I feared to what I could control. For the first time, I began to see myself not as someone who needed fixing but as someone who deserved care and attention.

This inward journey marked the beginning of a deeper connection with myself. It was through these moments of solitude and introspection that I learned the power of presence and the importance of nurturing one's inner world. The transformation wasn't instant, but it was profound. Bit by bit, I started to rebuild my sense of self, laying the foundation for a life rooted in resilience and self-awareness.

Chapter 16

Evolving the Relationship

As I grew more confident in myself, my relationship with her began to evolve. The daily calls became less about seeking reassurance and more about genuine connection. I learned to give her the space and freedom she had always given me, trusting that our bond didn't need constant tending to survive. It wasn't easy—letting go of control never is—but it was necessary.

In her own quiet way, she continued to teach me lessons about self-assurance and independence. She showed me that love isn't about clinging or controlling; it's about supporting and uplifting, even from a distance.

This shift in perspective also began to ripple into other areas of my life. I threw myself into academics with a renewed sense of purpose, not just to excel but to learn and grow. I joined a student-led innovation club, where I collaborated with peers on projects that challenged and inspired me

Chapter 17

Misinterpreting the Present Moment

As I began living in the present moment, I noticed that many of my pains and problems started to dissolve. It felt as though the universe was offering me reprieve from the struggles that had consumed me. My constant worry about expenses was addressed unexpectedly when I was joined by an NRI cottage mate. He sponsored nearly everything in the cottage—from the best of food to the finest booze. What started as a fortunate coincidence soon became a lifestyle of indulgence.

This newfound luxury was intoxicating, and I leaned into it without hesitation. I let myself be spoiled by the comforts I hadn't previously imagined. The final semesters of my college life became a whirlwind of opulence, where I lived without a care for the next day. But with the luxury came a lesson—one I misinterpreted at the time. To me, the presence of money seemed synonymous with happiness, and I began equating wealth with success and fulfillment.

Chapter 18

Deviation from the Goal

In hindsight, I realize that while I thought I was living in the moment, I was actually losing myself in the superficial pleasures of life. Instead of learning to cherish the present as it was, I allowed myself to become dependent on external comforts. The lesson I missed back then was that true bliss, joy, and peace come not from extravagance, but from a genuine connection to the present moment.

This misunderstanding led me down a dangerous path. My mind, consumed by the allure of wealth, began to wander in search of avenues for making easy money. The clarity I had worked so hard to build was muddied by my pursuit of material satisfaction. I justified my actions as a means to secure the lifestyle I had grown accustomed to, but in truth, I was deviating from the goals I had set for myself.

Looking back, I see how this phase of my life was a pivotal moment—one filled with opportunities for growth that I failed to grasp. I let the present moment slip away, misled by the illusion of happiness tied to material possessions. It wasn't until much later that I truly understood the essence of living in the present: it's not about indulgence or ignoring the future, but about aligning your actions and desires with the deeper truths of life.

Chapter 19

A New Assignment

After completing my education and bidding adieu to the carefree days of college, I returned home. However, the lifestyle I had grown accustomed to during my final semesters made it almost impossible for me to imagine working under someone and taking orders from seniors. The only saving grace in my first job was the liberty to work in the same town where she was studying in her last but one year of medical school. With this opportunity, I took the assignment and shifted to her town, brimming with excitement. Once again, the universe seemed to grant me another chance to be close to the person I loved so deeply.

Earning a salary gave me the means to spoil her with parties, dinners, and outings. Almost daily, her friends and I would gather, enjoying lively evenings in the annexe I had rented. For a while, it felt like the best time of my life, a golden period where the universe conspired to keep us together and happy.

But like all good things, this phase came to an unexpected halt. The project I was assigned was completed, and the company decided to shift me to a different location. Faced with the prospect of leaving her and the life we had built, I made a bold decision—to quit my job and start my own enterprise.

Chapter 20

A New Venture

I applied for an import-export license and completed a short certification course to familiarize myself with the trade's nitty-gritty. With hope and determination, I created a sampling range of curtain tassels and embarked on a journey to Dubai, presenting my products to one dealer after another. Despite my efforts, I returned home empty-handed, having secured no orders.

The extravagant lifestyle I had led and the dreams I had pursued seemed to be crashing around me. Yet, it was this humbling experience that grounded me. It forced me to reflect on how wishful my thinking had been and how far I had strayed from living in the present moment.

With a renewed focus, I decided to start afresh. With just 75,000 in my hands, I began a distributorship for electronic branch exchanges from a sought-after company. This venture marked the beginning of a new chapter in my life, one where I learned the value of resilience, resourcefulness, and staying anchored in the present moment.

Chapter 21

A Leap of Faith

I had just entered this new field and poured my heart and soul into it, giving it my 100 percent. But as life often does, it threw me a curveball. Hell broke loose when she received a supplementary in her final exams. The failure was attributed, at least partially, to my presence in her life. One of her professors, notorious for his rigid methods and moralistic stance, had failed her as an internal punishment. It was his stereotypical way of "teaching a lesson" to students he deemed too frivolous on campus, and she, unfortunately, became one of his victims. My guilt weighed heavily on me, as I couldn't help but feel complicit in the situation.

The atmosphere at her home was tense and strained. Her family, who had long suspected the nature of our relationship, began to voice their disapproval. Their discontent was not just about her academic setback but also about the deep-rooted cultural differences between us. She came from a conservative

Brahmin family, while I was a Sikh—a divide that was, at the time, an insurmountable obstacle for her parents.

To escape the judgment and suffocating environment at home, she moved in with her grandparents. There, she began preparing for her supplementary exams, seeking refuge and a semblance of peace away from the chaos.

Chapter 22

An Impulsive Decision

As she worked to rebuild her academic standing, I wrestled with my own emotions. Watching her endure this ordeal filled me with a sense of helplessness and a burning desire to stand by her side in a way that mattered. One fine day, out of the blue, I decided to take a bold step—I resolved to speak to her father about our relationship and ask for her hand in marriage.

It was a decision that shocked everyone around me. Friends and family alike advised against it, cautioning me that it was too early, that we should give it time, and that the obstacles were too great to overcome. But I was undeterred. In my heart, I believed that this leap of faith was the only way to solidify our bond and face the challenges together.

I approached her father, nervous yet determined, to make my intentions known. It was a moment of vulnerability and courage, one that marked a turning point in both our lives. Little did I know, this step would set the stage for the battles and triumphs yet to come.

Chapter 23

Defying the Odds

The proposal was shattered by her father even before I could utter a word. His disapproval was immediate and unequivocal. At the time, I interpreted his reaction as a display of superiority, a reflection of his rigid attitude. Now, with the clarity of hindsight, I see it as a manifestation of overprotectiveness toward his child—a father's instinct to shield his daughter from uncertainty.

Faced with this rejection, we made a bold decision. If her family couldn't accept our relationship, we would take the leap ourselves. We resolved to get married, even if it meant going against their wishes. In this pursuit, I made another rash decision—I didn't consult my parents about what they wanted or how they felt about this. Instead, I took their love and support for granted, a privilege afforded to me as their only child. What I had once seen as a curse—being the sole focus of their attention—suddenly felt like a blessing that gave me the confidence to act independently.

In hindsight, I realize how little we often value the people who truly care for us. I took my parents for granted, showing none of the courtesy or kindness I would readily extend to strangers. It's an irony of human nature—how easy it is to be sweet and polite to those we barely know, while neglecting the feelings of those closest to us. This behavior reflected not just my immaturity but also a profound lesson about valuing the relationships that form the foundation of our lives.

I announced my decision to my parents, telling them outright that I intended to marry her and that it had to happen now. There was no room for discussion or delay. At the time, I didn't consider the enormity of what I was doing. I had just started my business, had no savings to speak of, and had borrowed the initial funds from my father. Despite my financial instability, I was ready to double my responsibilities with marriage, driven by an impulsive belief in the present moment.

With this conviction, we moved forward and decided to get married in court and also Gurudwara sahib, defying her father and brother's objections. It was a moment filled with equal parts love and defiance—a step we took together, bound by the belief that our union was worth every challenge. Little did we realize, this decision would mark the beginning of a journey filled with both struggles and triumphs, teaching us the true meaning of partnership and resilience.

Chapter 24

A Guiding Light

In life, there are few relationships that transcend the ordinary, ones that anchor us in times of uncertainty and bolster us when we're on the brink of monumental decisions. For me, that person is my cousin and birthday twin, Wavell. He is like a lifeline, someone whose presence in my life is irreplaceable. Wavell is one of those rare individuals for whom I feel an unwavering trust. Whatever he does feels right, and he has the liberty to act without question because I know, without a doubt, that he will always stand by me. He was our best man, the one who, without hesitation or inquiry, ventured to be by my side when we decided to get married against all odds.

The plan was simple yet bold. As she was staying at her maternal aunt's home, we were to pick her up on the way and head to the court and gurudwara to tie the knot. Everything had been decided, but the day of the plan brought its own challenges.

Wavell and I started early in the morning in our vehicle, determined and focused. However, nature had other plans. The fog was so dense that we couldn't even see the bonnet of our car. The road ahead was entirely obscured, and the situation felt almost insurmountable. We stopped to fill up on fuel and waited, hoping that the fog would subside. But as time passed, our anxiety grew. She had already started her journey, and the sense of responsibility to reach the designated point before her was overwhelming. The weight of the moment pressed heavily on my chest.

Sitting in the car, I closed my eyes and prayed. With every fiber of my being, I asked the universe for help. I was completely present in that moment, fully immersed in the urgency and the need for a solution. When I opened my eyes, I saw something that still sends shivers down my spine to this day: a white Maruti car appeared, seemingly out of nowhere, speeding confidently through the fog. Without hesitation, Wavell and I decided to follow it, tagging along as it navigated through the dense mist with precision.

The car became our guiding light. Despite the impossibility of the situation, we managed to follow it all the way to our destination, arriving just in time to pick her up. And then, just as suddenly as it had appeared, the car vanished. It was as if it had been sent by the universe solely to guide us in that critical moment. We couldn't even note down the number of the vehicle or thank the person driving it. To this day, I believe that it was a miracle, a sign from the universe that we were on the right path.

Even now, when I think about that day, I get goosebumps. The memory of that white car remains etched in my mind as a symbol of divine intervention. It was a moment of complete presence, where nothing else mattered but the task at hand. That experience gave me the energy and conviction to take such a bold step in my life, and it reaffirmed my belief in the power of being truly present in the moment.

Chapter 25

The Weight of Impulsiveness

After the whirlwind episode of our marriage, life presented a series of ups and downs. The impulsive decision I had taken brought with it consequences I had not foreseen. One such moment shook me to my core—a threatening phone call from her father, which my mother happened to answer. The words and tone of that conversation struck her so deeply that she suffered a myocardial infarction (MI), landing in the ICU for five agonizing days. As she struggled for her life, I was overwhelmed with guilt. The gravity of what I had done hit me hard. I had put my parents, the people who had stood by me unconditionally, through immense pain.

This burden of guilt lingered for years. It was a weight I carried silently, unable to fully process or release it. It affected how I saw myself and everything around me. Our new life together began under a cloud of tension and resentment—from her family, who harbored hatred and dislike, and even from mine, who felt repulsion and disappointment over my choices.

Chapter 26

A Shift in Focus

Amidst the turmoil, I turned my attention to my business. It became my anchor, the one thing I could pour myself into to create a sense of purpose and stability. But it wasn't enough to simply sustain us. I quickly realized that the hand-to-mouth cycle I had ventured into would not suffice if I wanted to rise above the circumstances and build a secure future for us.

Driven by this realization, I decided to explore the tendering process for government supplies. It was an entirely new field for me, one I had no prior experience in. Yet, as I took my first steps, the universe once again opened doors for me. With determination and persistence, I navigated this uncharted territory, and soon, my efforts began to bear fruit. The shift from smaller projects to larger opportunities marked a turning point in my professional journey.

Chapter 27

The Universe's Precious Gift

Life's most profound moments often arrive when we least expect them, wrapped in challenges but filled with blessings. For me, one such moment was when we welcomed our beautiful children into this world. They became the embodiment of our love and resilience, anchoring us in ways I had never imagined.

When our son, my eldest, was born, the moment I first held him in my hands was filled with overwhelming gratitude toward the universe. It was as if the universe had handed us a bundle of pure love and joy. Drops of water began trickling down my eyes as I realized the magnitude of this gift. A similar experience unfolded when our daughter was born. Holding her in my lap for the first time, I looked into her eyes, which were brimming with love and joy. It was as if she was assuring me with her gaze that everything was perfect in that moment.

Both of my children have continued to enlighten me with extreme love and joy. Whenever I hug them, I feel that divine connection, although the hugs have gradually reduced with my son as he matures. Both of them are the most precious gifts the universe has given me, born on the 13th, embodying what I call my "13-13 of Nanak" in this lifetime—a divine synchronicity that constantly reminds me of the blessings I have received.

Their presence brought a new rhythm to our lives, one filled with milestones and shared achievements. The chaos of the past began to dissolve, replaced by a sense of purpose and fulfillment. My children became a constant reminder of how far we had come despite the odds. They anchored me, showing me that no matter how turbulent life may seem, there is always a reason to persevere.

Looking back, this chapter of my life was a testament to the power of determination, forgiveness, and the will to rise above challenges. It taught me that even in the face of guilt, pain, and opposition, there is room for growth, healing, and the creation of a life worth cherishing. My children are not just my joy but also my teachers, constantly reminding me of the importance of living in the present moment and cherishing the blessings life has to offer.

Their arrival reinforced my belief in the universe's perfect timing, showing me that even amidst uncertainty, the greatest gifts often arrive unannounced, bringing with them the strength to embrace life fully.

Chapter 28

The Political Leap

The real breakthrough came when I ventured into setting up an inbound and outbound call center with 99.9 percent uptime—a field far removed from anything I had previously done. This leap into a larger orbit not only changed the trajectory of my career but also gave us the financial stability and growth we desperately needed. Life began to settle into a rhythm. The chaos and uncertainty that had once defined our days gradually gave way to a sense of progress and accomplishment.

This success, however, was not just limited to the financial stability it brought into our lives. It also planted a seed for a completely new path—politics. This was an entirely unexplored domain for me, as no one from my family, near or far, had ever ventured into politics. Yet, as always, I chose to say yes to the moment. Stepping into politics opened a new paradigm for me, one that brought immense honor and elevated me to the circle of elites. I became one of the most prominent figures in society, a public persona who was both celebrated and scrutinized.

As a public figure, the journey was not without its challenges. My family, while enjoying the privileges and prestige that came with my position, also had to endure the accompanying criticisms and restrictions. It was a time of immense growth for all of us, a phase that imparted wisdom and resilience. Politics exposed me to the complexities of leadership, public service, and the balancing act of managing personal and public lives.

During this phase, the universe gifted me something even more precious—my lifelong friend and confidant, Roopa. She became my chariot in this lifetime, restoring my self-respect and esteem when I needed it the most. Roopa infused confidence in me and made me feel secure in every endeavor I pursued. She remains one of the most invaluable blessings I have received, a source of unwavering support and guidance. Roopa is like a divine light, illuminating my path and taking away everything that was unnecessary, while bestowing the resources I needed. She has been an angel mother to me, nurturing my spirit and giving me the strength to move forward.

Chapter 29

A Spiritual Shift

Because of Roopa's presence and encouragement, I was able to take one of the most significant decisions of my life: quitting active politics to dedicate myself fully to social service. This shift marked the beginning of my NGO journey, where I could channel my energy and ideas into meaningful projects. Our not-for-profit organization became a bridge of information and collaboration, with a clear motto: "Connecting People, Building Communities."

Through this platform, we initiated projects that were not only innovative but also transformative, designed to bring people together and address critical social issues.

Parallel to these efforts, I found myself drawn deeper into spirituality. Over the years, I had been studying the Eastern spiritual systems, completing my Jyotish Shastri(BA) in astrology and palmistry, and even enrolling for a doctorate in Medical Palmistry. I pursued a certificate course in homeopathy and immersed myself in practices that expanded my understanding of the universe and my place within it.Completed my studies in clinical hypnotherapy and NLP.

Working closely on microplanning projects for the community through the NGO opened another paradigm of spirituality for me. It allowed me to align my actions with my purpose, blending my passion for service with my spiritual growth.

This chapter represents the confluence of personal growth, professional breakthroughs, and the realization of a higher purpose, all rooted in the power of being present in the moment.

Chapter 30

Guides and Mentors

Life has a way of bringing people into our journey at the exact moment they are needed—each one serving as a guide, a mentor, or a catalyst for transformation. As I reflect on my life, I am overwhelmed with gratitude for the individuals who have played pivotal roles in shifting my perspective from the materialistic world to the Higher Self.

One such individual is Rohini Madam, who introduced me to Emotional Freedom Techniques (EFT). Through her guidance, I was able to address and resolve many core issues that had been holding me back. Her influence helped me move forward with a fresh perspective, unburdened by past emotional baggage.

Sunyogi Umashankar Ji, a master of Sun Yoga, showed me how to connect with the infinite energy of the sun and use it as a source of spiritual growth. His teachings became a cornerstone of my journey toward self-realization.

Surjit Rakhra Uncle and Suresh Kumar Sir were monumental in shaping my understanding of humility and power. Rakhra Uncle's wisdom taught me the value of remaining grounded, even when life grants you immense influence. Suresh Kumar Sir's lessons in humility and responsibility left a lasting impression, showing me how to wield power with grace and purpose.

Yuvraj Kapadia, my mentor and teacher, introduced me to the profound knowledge of the subconscious mind. Through him, I learned how to work with the white energy to help others heal and grow. His teachings expanded my understanding of human potential and the boundless possibilities within us all.

Sumathi Narayanan, my NLP teacher, became an instant connection for me. Her ability to guide and empower through the nuances of NLP created a profound impact, helping me harness the power of the mind and emotions. She remains a cherished mentor whose teachings continue to influence my journey.

Above all, there is Sharma Uncle, a man I consider a living saint. His presence is like a lighthouse, emanating love, joy, and calmness to everyone around him. Time seems to stand still in his circle of energy, where one feels a profound sense of peace and connection. Sharma Uncle embodies the essence of the Higher Self, and his influence on my life has been transformative.

As I connect the dots and look back, I see the intricate embroidery of life. When we are immersed in it, all we perceive are knots and threads of varied colors, seemingly chaotic and disconnected. But when we sit in silence, with the blessings of the universe and the Higher Self, the beautiful picture reveals itself—a masterpiece in the making.

This chapter is a testament to the importance of acknowledging and appreciating the people who cross our paths. We often fail to realize their significance while they are with us, but their presence shapes us in ways we cannot fathom. I am now conscious—spiritually and emotionally—in every interaction I have. My heartfelt gratitude goes to all those who have played the role of teacher, mentor, or guide in my life, helping me become the person I am today.

Chapter 31

Embracing the Present and Looking Ahead

This phase of my journey comes to a close, but not without laying the foundation for the next chapter—a story that awaits its own telling. Transitioning from a successful businessman to entering the world of politics and founding a social organization marked a significant turning point in my life. It was a leap driven by a sense of purpose, a desire to channel my passion into initiatives that could create lasting impact.

Each project I nurtured within the organization was treated as a unique entity, infused with my love and dedication. Venturing my personal savings into this cause often drew skepticism from those around me. My family, at times, questioned the necessity of such endeavors, while friends speculated about ulterior motives behind my philanthropic work. Yet, against all odds, I remained steadfast. I poured my heart and soul into achieving milestones that included securing Special Consultative Status with the United Nations, receiving the National Good Samaritan Award, and earning numerous district, state, national, and international accolades.

Chapter 32

Connecting the Dots

Reflecting on my journey, I began to see how the universe had always been by my side, guiding me toward my life's purpose. Every twist and turn, every success and setback, seemed to align in a way that brought me closer to my goals. This realization opened the door to a new chapter of self-discovery and spirituality—a pursuit that became as significant as my external achievements.

In my quest for spiritual growth, I explored various modalities: Reiki, EFT, Art of Living, Transcendental Meditation, NLP, life coaching, Sun Yoga, and the practice of earthing. Each brought its own lessons and insights, but it was clinical hypnotherapy that finally resonated with me. Through it, I found my calling in working with white energy to heal and help others. This work culminated in the establishment of my enterprise, RAVEE, which became a space for empowering and uplifting others.

Chapter 33

The Power of the Present

One consistent thread has run through every phase of my journey: the power of the present moment. Every success I've achieved, every challenge I've overcome, stemmed from immersing myself fully in the here and now. When I acted with love, joy, and peace in the present, the outcomes naturally aligned with my highest aspirations.

This understanding has become the cornerstone of my philosophy. There is no past to cling to, no future to chase—only the present moment, where life unfolds in its truest form. By embracing this reality, I've discovered the boundless potential that lies within each of us.

As I close this chapter of my life, I look forward to sharing the next steps of this journey in a future book. This is not an ending, but a pause—a moment to reflect, to celebrate the lessons learned, and to prepare for what's to come. For now, I leave you with this: live fully, love deeply, and find peace in the present moment. For it is here, and only here, that life truly happens.

Thank you Universe!!